Learning Latin
Through Mythology

Jayne I. Hanlin
Beverly E. Lichtenstein

CAMBRIDGE
UNIVERSITY PRESS

Published by the Press Syndicate of the University of Cambridge
The Pitt Building, Trumpington Street, Cambridge CB2 1RP
40 West 20th Street, New York, NY 10011–4211, USA
10 Stamford Road, Oakleigh, Melbourne 3166, Australia

First published 1991
Reprinted 1995

Printed in Great Britain by Bell and Bain Ltd., Glasgow

British Library cataloguing in publication data
Hanlin, Jayne I.
    Learning Latin through mythology.
    1. Latin language
    I. Title   II. Lichtenstein, Beverly E.
    470

Library of Congress cataloging in publication data applied for

ISBN 0 521 397790

Cover and text illustrations by Hemesh Alles
Picture research by Callie Kendall

DS

Acknowledgements
Thanks are due to the following for permission to reproduce photographs:
p.11 The Mansell Collection; p.36 E.K. Thompson/Aquila Photographics.

Contents

Parts of all of the above sections are recorded on the accompanying cassette, which is available separately (ISBN 0 521 40762 1).

Atalanta and Hippomenes

Atalanta had been warned never to marry. Whenever young men came wishing to marry her, Atalanta would challenge them to a foot race. She made sure she always won and the losers were put to death.

While Hippomenes was judging these races, he was overcome by Atalanta's beauty and fell in love with her.

Hippomenes prayed to the goddess Venus for help. She gave him three golden apples with instructions to drop the apples, one at a time, at Atalanta's feet to distract her as they raced. When Atalanta stopped to pick up the last apple, Hippomenes sped past her and claimed the victory.

Atalanta married Hippomenes. But in their happiness, they forgot to thank Venus for their good fortune. Enraged, she caused them to offend the goddess Cybele, who changed them into lions and made them pull her chariot ever after.

Atalanta et Hippomenēs

A Hippomenēs erat iūdex.
semper Atalanta celerrimē currēbat.

B Atalanta semper erat victrīx.
sī iuvenis nōn erat victor iūdicēs iuvenem
interficiēbant.

C Hippomenēs deam laudāvit.
Venus eī tria māla aurea dedit.

D Hippomenēs māla ēmīsit.
Atalanta māla īnspexit.

E Hippomenēs igitur erat victor. euge !

F Atalanta tamen et Hippomenēs Venerī
grātiās nōn ēgērunt.
Atalanta igitur erat lea et Hippomenēs
erat leō.

aurea	*golden*	iūdex/iūdicēs	*judge/s*
celerrimē	*fastest*	iuvenis/iuvenem	*young man*
currēbat	*used to run*	laudāvit	*praised*
deam	*goddess*	lea	*lioness*
dedit	*gave*	leō	*lion*
eī	*to him*	māla	*apples*
ēmīsit	*dropped*	nōn	*not*
erat	*was*	semper	*always*
et	*and*	sī	*if*
euge!	*hurrah!*	tamen	*however*
grātiās ēgērunt	*gave thanks*	tria	*three*
igitur	*therefore*	victor/victrīx	*winner*
īnspexit	*looked at*	Venerī	*to Venus*
interficiēbant	*killed*		

●   Translate each sentence and then match it with the correct picture.

____ rhētor *puerō* stilum trādidit.

____ nauta *mercātōrī* pecūniam trādidit.

____ poēta *āctōrī* versum ostendit.

____ māter *puellae* librum ostendit.

____ coquus *amīcō* pāvōnem offerēbat.

____ pistor *columbae* pānem offerēbat.

____ pater *fīliae* ānulum dedit.

____ Apollō *victōrī* laurum dedit.

āctōrī	*to the actor*	pānem	*bread*
amīcō	*to the friend*	pater	*father*
ānulum	*ring*	pāvōnem	*peacock*
columbae	*to the dove*	pecūniam	*money*
coquus	*cook*	pistor	*baker*
dedit	*gave*	poēta	*poet*
fīliae	*to the daughter*	puellae	*to the girl*
laurum	*laurel crown*	puerō	*to the boy*
librum	*book*	rhētor	*teacher*
māter	*mother*	stilum	*stylus*
mercātōrī	*to the merchant*	trādidit	*handed over*
nauta	*sailor*	versum	*verse*
offerēbat	*was offering*	victōrī	*to the victor*
ostendit	*showed*		

●   Designing a board game is lots of fun. Since Atalanta and Hippomenes raced against each other, making a "path" game would be an activity in the spirit of the myth. You will need a stiff piece of cardboard, crayons or markers, a set of dice, and some kind of game pieces to move. Although Atalanta and Hippomenes are the two main characters in the myth, you might include other suitors in the race. You must also decide on a prize for the winner. Perhaps you could make a golden apple or a cardboard trophy for the victor.

Draw a winding path. Mark off boxes at regular intervals on the path. Indicate the "Start" and "Finish" points on the board. In each of the boxes write a direction that will either help or hinder the progress of the racers. Some ideas are:

1. You trip over a rock on the path. Lose one turn.
2. Venus gives wings to your feet. Speed ahead two boxes.
3. A terrible rainstorm turns the path into a sea of mud. Go back three boxes.

You will be able to think of lots of clever directions to put on your game board. For example, you might include a golden apple on several squares with the direction "Lose a turn." You can even change the directions in the boxes by writing new ones on gummed labels and pasting them over the originals.

To play the game, roll the dice. The person with the highest number starts the game. The other players will follow in the order of their roll. The first player rolls the dice, moves his or her marker the number of boxes indicated on the dice, and follows the directions in the box. Each player follows in turn. The first person to reach the "Finish" is the winner. This is just one set of sample directions. You may make up your own for more challenging games. Enjoy playing!

●   Using three golden apples any way you wish, plan a relay race for your friends. Write the directions clearly, step by step.

Baucis and Philemon

Baucis and Philemon were a poor, elderly couple. Baucis loved to work in her kitchen while Philemon enjoyed his garden.

One day two strangers arrived at their door. Baucis and Philemon invited the strangers into the kitchen and offered them food and drink. There on the table was boiled cabbage stew, olives, cheese, wine, apples and wild honey. The strangers ate and drank everything in sight! But, to Baucis and Philemon's amazement, the wine never ran out.

The strangers were really Jupiter and Mercury in disguise. When the old couple discovered this, they tried to catch their goose and serve it to the gods. But the goose got away!

As a reward for Baucis and Philemon's generosity, Jupiter made their cottage a temple and made them its guardians. He also granted their wish to remain together after death by changing them into trees. Forever after their branches entwined.

Baucis et Philēmōn

A Baucis in culīnā labōrat.
Philēmōn in hortō labōrat.

B Iuppiter intrat et circumspectat.
Mercurius intrat et circumspectat.

C cibus et vīnum sunt in mēnsā.

D Iuppiter sedet et bibit.
Mercurius sedet et bibit.

bibit	*drinks*	in mēnsā	*on the table*
cibus	*food*	intrat	*enters*
circumspectat	*looks around*	labōrat	*works*
et	*and*	sedet	*sits*
in culīnā	*in the kitchen*	sunt	*are*
in hortō	*in the garden*	vīnum	*wine*

• Baucis and Philemon offered various foods to their guests. Read about them in the list of words and phrases. Then select the correct Latin sentences for each picture.

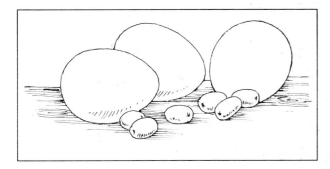

brassica est in mēnsā.

nucēs sunt in mēnsā.

oleae sunt in mēnsā.

cāseus est in mēnsā.

mel est in mēnsā.

mālum est in mēnsā.

vīnum est in mēnsā.

ōva sunt in mēnsā.

brassica	*cabbage*	nucēs	*nuts*
cāseus	*cheese*	oleae	*olives*
est	*is*	ōva	*eggs*
in mēnsā	*on the table*	sunt	*are*
mālum	*apple*	vīnum	*wine*
mel	*honey*		

but the ___ got away!

ānser

- The list of words and phrases in the previous activity contains some of the food Baucis and Philemon served Jupiter and Mercury. On a paper plate draw these foods (or cut them out of coloured paper) and label them in Latin.

- Look at some pictures of Roman temples. Make a list of the most important elements, such as "pediment," "architrave," "column," and "frieze." For each of these words write an English sentence using alliteration – so that all the important words begin with the same letter. Then illustrate each of your sentences. For example:
Perseus perched precariously on the pediment of the Pantheon.

- Imagine your house has been turned into a Roman temple just like in the story. Draw a picture of your house or bring in a photograph. Using an acetate overlay and coloured markers, transform your house into a Roman temple.

Cephalus and Procris

Cephalus adored his wife Procris. Because Cephalus liked to hunt, Procris gave him two gifts from the goddess Diana—a dog so fast he never failed to catch his prey and a javelin which always hit its mark.

After hunting, Cephalus was in the habit of calling Aura, the breeze, to cool and refresh him. One day someone overheard Cephalus and, suspecting he had a lover, told Procris. The next morning she followed Cephalus and hid in the bushes. When she heard him speaking lovingly, she sighed. Thinking it was an animal, Cephalus threw the javelin which Procris had given him and killed his beloved wife. Alas! He had only been talking to the breeze.

Cephalus et Procris

A Cephalus est vēnātor.

B Cephalus canem et vēnābulum habet.

C Cephalus in silvā recumbit et clāmat.

D Procris Cephalum audit.
Procris lacrimat.

audit	*hears*	in silvā	*in the woods*
canem	*dog*	lacrimat	*cries*
clāmat	*calls out*	recumbit	*lies down*
est	*is*	vēnābulum	*hunting spear*
et	*and*	vēnātor	*hunter*
habet	*has*		

decem	*ten*	quīnque	*five*
duo	*two*	trēs	*three*
quadrāgintā	*forty*	trīgintā	*thirty*
quīndecim	*fifteen*	ūnus	*one*
quīnquāgintā	*fifty*	vīgintī	*twenty*

●   Using the list of words and phrases, write in the correct Latin word after each numeral.

I _____   XX _____

II _____   XL _____

III_____   XV _____

V _____   L   _____

X _____   XXX_____

●   Here are the Roman numerals from one to twenty:

I	XI
II	XII
III	XIII
IV	XIV
V	XV
VI	XVI
VII	XVII
VIII	XVIII
IX	XIX
X	XX

Following the correct sequence of numbers, join the dots below to make a picture.

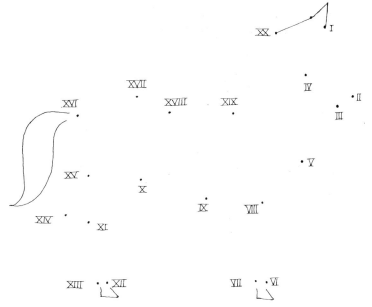

Now make up your own dot-to-dot picture, using Roman numerals. Give it to a classmate to join the dots.

●   Procris gave a special pet to Cephalus—a swift hunting dog. Think of all the reasons that made this a special pet. What do you think it could do that an ordinary hunting dog could not do? Record your answer in comic strip form.
    Now think about a pet that you have or would like to have. What special qualities do you think this pet has or should have? Record your answer in comic strip form.

●   Some people say that pets make life more pleasant for older people who cannot leave their home. Do you agree? Explain your answer.

Daedalus and Icarus

King Minos asked Daedalus, a famous architect and inventor, to construct a labyrinth for him. However, soon after the maze was completed, the king became angry with Daedalus and shut him and his son, Icarus, in a tower on an island. They were unable to get away by land or sea. But Daedalus was determined to escape and used his skills to make wings for himself and Icarus by joining feathers with thread and wax. When he attached the wings to each of their arms, they rose into the sky.

"Fly close by me," Daedalus warned his son. "If you soar too high, the sun will melt the wax; if you swoop too low, the sea will make the feathers wet."

Daedalus flew safely to Sicily, but Icarus did not obey his father's instructions and soared too close to the sun. The sun melted the wax, the feathers fell off, and the boy plunged into the sea.

Daedalus et Īcarus

A Daedalus et Īcarus dē vītā iamdūdum dēspērābant.

B Daedalus cēram et pennās parāvit.

C postrēmō Daedalus per aurās ēvolāvit. Īcarus per aurās paulīsper ēvolāvit.

D Daedalus circumspectāvit. "ēheu!" exclāmāvit trīstis Daedalus, "Īcarus est mortuus."

cēram	*wax*	mortuus	*dead*
circumspectāvit	*looked all around*	parāvit	*prepared*
dē vītā dēspērābant	*were despairing for their life*	paulīsper	*for a short time*
ēheu!	*alas!*	pennās	*feathers*
est	*is*	per aurās ēvolāvit	*flew through the air*
et	*and*	postrēmō	*finally*
exclāmāvit	*called out*	trīstis	*sad*
iamdūdum	*long ago*		

B

āctor	*actor*	mercātor	*merchant*
agricola	*farmer*	nauta	*sailor*
architectus	*architect*	palaestrā	*exercise ground*
argentāriā	*banker's stall*	pistor	*baker*
argentārius	*banker*	pistrīnā	*bakery*
āthlēta	*athlete*	portū	*harbor*
basilicā	*court building*	scaenā	*stage*
est	*is*	sellā	*chair*
fūnambulus	*tightrope walker*	silvā	*forest*
fundō	*farm*	tabernā	*shop*
in	*in; on*	theātrō	*theater*
īnstitor	*peddler, tradesman*	vēnātor	*hunter*
iūdex	*judge*	viā	*street*

● Using the vocabulary above match each Latin sentence below to its correct picture.

_____ nauta est in portū.

_____ fūnambulus est in theātrō.

_____ agricola est in fundō.

_____ architectus est in sellā.

_____ āctor est in scaenā.

_____ āthlēta est in palaestrā.

_____ vēnātor est in silvā.

_____ īnstitor est in viā.

_____ pistor est in pistrīnā.

_____ iūdex est in basilicā.

_____ mercātor est in tabernā.

_____ argentārius est in argentāriā.

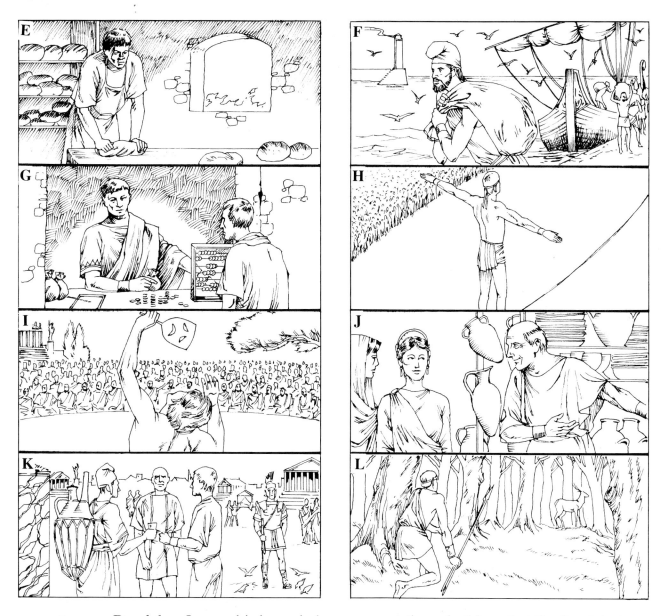

- Daedalus, Icarus, birds, and planes are not the only things that fly. Look in magazines to find different things that fly. Be creative! Then cut out the pictures, paste them on heavy paper, and make a collage. (A collage is an assortment of overlapping pictures, cut into interesting shapes and pasted onto a background, with no empty spaces.) When you finish, you may wish to cut the collage in the shape of something that flies.

- Daedalus was very clever to make wings out of feathers, string, and wax. Imagine you are trapped on an island. You have only one wheel, a large ball of string, a large box of chewing gum, and one item of your choice (**or** a stylus, a shield, a pile of logs, and one item of your choice). What would you construct to make your escape? Write about it, illustrate, and share it.

  Suppose you were marooned on an island with one of the people from the list of people in the activity on the previous page. Whom would you choose to help you escape? Why?

Daphne and Apollo

Daphne was a beautiful nymph, and she loved to run through the forest. One day the powerful god Apollo saw her and began to pursue her. Daphne at once fled, with Apollo at her heels.

Daphne ran to her father Peneus, who was a river god, and cried out in terror, "Please help me, father! Change my form or let the earth swallow me!"

As Apollo reached out to touch her, his fingers felt a woody trunk. Her arms were now branches, her hair green leaves and where her feet had been grew immovable roots. Daphne had turned into a beautiful laurel tree.

Daphnē et Apollō

A Apollō est deus potēns.

B Daphnē est nympha.
Daphnē in silvā habitat.

C Apollō Daphnēn amat.
Daphnē fugit.

D Daphnē est laurus.

amat	*loves*	in	*in*
deus potēns	*powerful god*	laurus	*laurel tree*
est	*is*	nympha	*nymph*
fugit	*runs away*	silvā	*woods*
habitat	*lives*		

Quid est? (What is it?)

———————

———————

———————

• Label each picture with the appropriate Latin words, chosen from the list below.

caelum	*sky*	nūbēs	*cloud*
flūmen	*river*	piscīna	*fishpond*
fūmus	*smoke*	silva	*woods, forest*
incendium	*fire*	sōl	*sun*
lūna	*moon*	stēlla	*star*
mōns	*mountain*	terra	*ground*

●   *Concentration* is a card game that is easy to make. First of all, fold twelve 3″ × 5″ index cards in half. On the left side write a Latin word from the list on p.22; on the right side draw a picture for the Latin word. Then cut each card on the fold.

    Now you are ready to play. The object of the game is to match as many Latin words with their pictures as you can.

Directions
1. One player shuffles the cards and spreads them face down.
2. The first player turns two cards over.
3. If they match, the player keeps the pair and takes another turn.
4. If they do not match, the player turns them back over where he or she found them.
5. The next player begins with step 2.
6. Play continues until all of the cards have been matched.
7. The player with the most pairs is the winner.

(You might also wish to play with Latin names for animals, using the vocabulary in *Diana and Actaeon* p.26.)

●   Do you think Daphne was happy as a tree? If *you* had been her father, what form would you have given her? Explain your answers.

Diana and Actaeon

One day Actaeon was out hunting with his dogs. By chance, he wandered to the goddess Diana's cave and saw her bathing. Unable to reach for an arrow to shoot at Actaeon, the angry goddess threw water in his face. Quick as a wink, antlers grew out of Actaeon's forehead; his ears became pointed and his neck grew longer; his arms turned into long legs and his hands became hooves. Soon his whole body was covered with a spotted hide. When he caught his reflection in a stream, he saw that he had turned into a stag.

Actaeon's hunting dogs did not recognize their master, when they spied the stag running through the forest. The well-trained animals pursued their master and tore him to pieces. Diana's anger was thus appeased.

Diāna et Actaeōn

A Actaeōn vēnātur.

B Actaeōn Diānam videt.

C Diāna aquam iactat.

D Actaeōn ē cavernā currit.
nunc Actaeōn est cervus.

aqua/aquam	*water*	iactat	*throws*
cervus	*stag*	nunc	*now*
currit	*runs*	vēnātur	*hunts*
ē cavernā	*out of the cave*	videt	*sees*

- Read the sentences below and match each picture with the correct sentence. The first one has been done for you.

C canis lātrat.	____ canis custōdit.
____ fēlēs bibit.	____ columba ēvolat.
____ leō fremit.	____ pāvō stat.
____ lupus cervum agitat.	____ fēlēs dormit.
____ cervus currit.	____ asinus labōrat.

asinus	*donkey*	agitat	*hunts*
canis	*dog*	bibit	*drinks*
cervus/cervum	*deer*	currit	*runs*
columba	*dove*	custōdit	*guards*
fēlēs	*cat*	dormit	*sleeps*
leō	*lion*	ēvolat	*flies away*
lupus	*wolf*	fremit	*roars*
pāvō	*peacock*	labōrat	*works*
		lātrat	*barks*
		stat	*stands*

- Make a "flip book" to show how Actaeon changed from a hunter to a stag. Here's how:

    1. Cut 14 pieces of thick 3″ × 5″ paper or use 3″ × 5″ index cards.
    2. Draw a succession of 13 pictures (one on each piece of paper) starting with Actaeon as a hunter and ending with Actaeon as a stag.
    3. Staple together and make a cover.
    4. As you read other myths, you might try making other mythological flip books. For example, you might show Baucis and Philemon becoming trees, Narcissus becoming a flower, the beautiful woman Medusa becoming a Gorgon, Daphne becoming a laurel tree, or Atalanta and Hippomenes becoming a lioness and a lion.

- Many animals go through changes before they become an adult. Find out what changes these animals go through before becoming an adult: butterfly, frog, praying mantis. Write about the changes, make an illustration, and share your work. Select two more animals of your choice to write about and illustrate in the same way.
- Compare the story of Diana and Actaeon to reality. What things could not have happened? Why?
    ○ If you had been Actaeon, what would you have done and why?
    ○ If you had been Diana, what would you have done and why?

Echo and Narcissus

Echo was a forest nymph who had been punished by the goddess Juno for talking too much. She was no longer able to use her voice, except to repeat the last words that others spoke.

One day, the beautiful young Narcissus was resting in the forest after the hunt. As soon as Echo caught sight of him, she fell in love. When Narcissus called his companions to join him, Echo—thinking he was calling her—repeated his last words, "Join me" and rushed out to meet him. But Narcissus rejected her, and Echo pined away until all that was left of her was her voice.

Narcissus, however, was also fated to suffer an unrequited love. Kneeling by a pool to refresh himself, he fell in love with his own reflection. The love, of course, could never be returned, and he died of a broken heart. Out of pity, Jupiter changed him into a beautiful flower, called the narcissus.

Ēchō et Narcissus

A Ēchō nympha est in silvā.
Narcissus est vēnātor.

B Ēchō Narcissum amat.
ēheu! ēheu!

C Narcissus clāmat.
Ēchō respondet.

D Narcissus prope aquam iacet.
Narcissus imāginem videt.

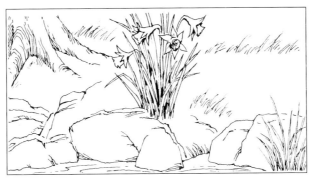

E Narcissus fit parvus flōs.

amat	*loves, likes*	in silvā	*in the woods*
clāmat	*calls*	nympha	*nymph*
ēheu!	*alas!*	parvus	*small*
est	*is*	prope aquam	*near the water*
fit	*becomes*	respondet	*replies*
flōs	*flower*	vēnātor	*hunter*
iacet	*rests*	videt	*sees*
imāginem	*image, reflection*		

- In English, the word order changes the meaning of a sentence. For example, "Echo loves Narcissus" has a different meaning from "Narcissus loves Echo." In Latin, the word ending indicates the meaning. Look at the example opposite.

The ending shows that Narcissus is receiving the action, not doing it.

amīcus *dōnum* amat.   spectātor _____ amat.

gladiātor _____ amat.   dea _____ amat.

frāter _____ amat.   māter _____ amat.

nauta _____ amat.   tōnsor _____ amat.

Use the Latin words below to fill in the blanks. The first one has been done for you.

āctōrem   arēnam   deum   dōnum

īnfantem   nāvem   novāculam   sorōrem

āctor	*actor*	īnfāns	*baby, child*
amīcus	*friend*	māter	*mother*
arēna	*arena*	nauta	*sailor*
dea	*goddess*	nāvis	*ship*
deus	*god*	novācula	*razor*
dōnum	*gift*	soror	*sister*
frāter	*brother*	spectātor	*spectator*
gladiātor	*gladiator*	tōnsor	*barber*

- Many flowers like the narcissus have Latin or mythological derivations. Using a dictionary and an encyclopedia, find out more about the flowers listed below. Make a booklet with illustrations and interesting facts about each flower.

amaryllis   aster   columbine   gladiolus
hyacinth   iris   narcissus   nasturtium

Can you think of any other plants to add to your booklet?

Ēchō Narciss*um* amat.
Echo loves Narcissus.

Quis Sum? *(Who Am I?)*

●   Look at the illustrations and English sentences below. Then select the correct Latin sentence for each from the list below.

A I am the god who throws thunderbolts.

B I was changed into a laurel tree.

C I drove my father's sun chariot.

D Everything I touched turned to gold.

E I am a flying horse.

F I was changed into a stag.

G My husband and I became trees.

H I fell in love with my reflection.

I I disobeyed and flew too close to the sun.

J I gave my husband Diana's gifts.

K Jupiter changed me into a cow.

L I lost a race because of three golden apples.

M I was chained to a rock.

N I killed Medusa.

O I was turned into a lion.

P Only my voice remains.

Atalanta sum.	Daphnē sum.	Pēgasus sum.	Phaëthōn sum.
Procris sum.	Īcarus sum.	Actaeōn sum.	Perseus sum.
Īō sum.	Iuppiter sum.	Baucis sum.	Hippomenēs sum.
Midas sum.	Andromeda sum.	Narcissus sum.	Ēchō sum.

C

Io

Jupiter once fell in love with the beautiful nymph Io. To protect her from Juno's anger he changed her into a cow. But Juno claimed the cow as a gift and promptly handed her over to Argus for safe-keeping.

Argus was a creature with one hundred eyes, who was able to guard Io night and day. While each pair of eyes took its turn sleeping, the other ninety-eight were firmly fixed on Io, tied to an olive tree.

Jupiter felt sorry for Io and sent his messenger Mercury to help her. Mercury sang so sweetly that one by one, all Argus's eyes closed and he fell asleep. Mercury cut off Argus's head and freed Io.

Argus had been a favourite of Juno. The goddess was so upset that she took each one of Argus's eyes and put it on the peacock, her favourite bird. Now, one hundred eyes look at you when a peacock spreads its tail.

Īō

A Argus Īō dīligenter custōdit.

B Mercurius est callidus et suāviter cantat.

C mox Argus dormit.
  Mercurius Argum celeriter necat.

D nunc oculī Argī sunt in pāvōne.

callidus	*clever*	in pāvōne	*on the peacock*
cantat	*sings*	mox	*soon*
celeriter	*quickly*	necat	*kills*
custōdit	*guards*	nunc	*now*
dīligenter	*diligently*	oculī	*eyes*
dormit	*sleeps*	suāviter	*sweetly*
est	*is*	sunt	*are*
et	*and*		

• Fill in the blanks in the following sentences with the appropriate Latin adverbs from the list below. Some sentences may have more than one answer.

I pāvō ＿＿＿＿＿＿ ambulat.   **II** pāvō ＿＿＿＿＿＿ pānem cōnsūmit.

III pāvō ＿＿＿＿＿＿ clāmitat.   **IV** pāvō ＿＿＿＿＿＿ stat.

V pāvō ＿＿＿＿＿＿ fugit.   **VI** pāvō ＿＿＿＿＿＿ recumbit.

ambulat	*walks*	cautē	*cautiously*
clāmitat	*screams*	celeriter	*quickly*
cōnsūmit	*eats*	magnificē	*splendidly*
fugit	*runs away*	subitō	*suddenly*
pānem	*bread*	tacitē	*quietly*
pāvō	*peacock*	timidē	*fearfully*
recumbit	*lies down*		
stat	*stands*		

- Design a mosaic of Juno's favourite bird, the peacock. Here's how:

  1. Draw an outline of your picture on heavy paper.
  2. Choose a variety of different paper – different colours, different textures (including shiny) – and cut them up into small pieces. Then stick the pieces down inside the outline of your picture.
  3. Be sure to cover the background as well as the peacock.

- Pretend you are Mercury. Write a story (or compose a song) that would put Argus to sleep. Tape your story (or song).

King Midas

When the god Bacchus granted king Midas a wish, the king asked that everything he touched would turn to gold. How happy he was at first! A twig, a stone, a clod of dirt, even the palace pillars all turned to gold. But when he tried to eat and drink, he found that golden food and drink did not satisfy his hunger and thirst.

So Midas asked Bacchus to forgive his foolishness. Bacchus told him to climb to the source of the river Pactolus and jump in. Midas freed himself of his golden touch, but the river still has a golden tinge to this day.

Midas

A Midas aurum amat.
omnia sunt aurea.

B Midas ēsurit.
cibus est aureus.

C Midas nōn est laetus.
Midas vīnum nōn bibit.
Midas cibum nōn cōnsūmit.

D nunc aurum in flūmine est.
Midas grātiās agit.

amat	*loves*	grātiās agit	*gives thanks*
aurea/aureus	*golden*	in flūmine	*in the river*
aurum	*gold*	laetus	*happy*
bibit	*is drinking*	nōn	*not*
cibus/cibum	*food*	nunc	*now*
cōnsūmit	*is eating*	omnia	*all things*
est	*is*	sunt	*are*
ēsurit	*is hungry*	vīnum	*wine*

• Each pair of Latin adjectives below shows two opposite meanings. Match the appropriate adjective with each picture on p.41. Then draw your own picture to illustrate the other adjective in each pair. Label them in Latin.

vetus	*old*	fēlīx	*lucky*
novus	*new*	īnfēlīx	*unlucky*
ignāvus	*lazy*	īrātus	*angry*
occupātus	*busy*	laetus	*happy*
magnus	*big*	prīmus	*first*
parvus	*small*	ultimus	*last*

- Draw a beautiful garden. Then, using a yellow crayon, draw the same garden to show how it looked after King Midas changed everything to gold or overlay your original drawing with gold cellophane.

- Compare and contrast your two gardens. What would life be like if everything and everyone in our world were the same? Some think "variety is the spice of life." Do you agree or disagree? Why?

Pegasus and Bellerophon

Bellerophon was given the task of killing the Chimaera, a terrible fire-breathing monster who was destroying the land. While Bellerophon slept before setting out, the goddess Minerva placed a golden bridle at his side. When he awoke, Bellerophon saw Pegasus, a wonderful winged horse. How he wanted to ride him! He put the bridle on Pegasus, mounted him, and flew into the sky. In the distance Bellerophon caught sight of the Chimaera. He swooped low and cut off the monster's head.

Later, Bellerophon tried to ride Pegasus to Mount Olympus, the home of the gods. Jupiter was so angry that he sent a gadfly to sting Pegasus. Bellerophon was thrown and fell to earth.

Pēgasus

A Pēgasus est equus mīrābilis.

B Bellerophōn Chimaeram cōnspicit.

C hērōs est fortissimus.
hērōs mōnstrum petit.

D hērōs Chimaeram gladiō necat.

cōnspicit	*catches sight of*	hērōs	*hero*
equus	*horse*	mīrābilis	*wonderful*
est	*is*	mōnstrum	*monster*
fortissimus	*very brave*	necat	*kills*
gladiō	*with a sword*	petit	*attacks*

•   The following English adjectives come from Latin; they derive from Latin roots and are called *derivatives*. Use your dictionary to match each English derivative with the correct picture, and complete the English phrase.

asinine   canine   equine

feline   leonine   serpentine

I   like a   _____   **IV** like a   _____

II   like a   _____   **V**   like a   _____

III like a   _____   **VI** like a   _____

•   Now that you know the story of Pegasus, you can easily answer the first two mythological equations below. Using reference books, complete the other equations with the given answers. Then write your own mythological equation.

centaur	Chimaera	Harpy	minotaur
Cerberus	griffin	Medusa	Pegasus

1. horse + wings = _____

2. lion + goat + snake = _____

3. monstrous woman + bird = _____

4. lion + eagle = _____

5. bull + man = _____

6. horse + man = _____

7. dog + three heads = _____

8. woman + snaky hair = _____

•   Change your name into Latin. Then put it into the following headline and write a news story.

Ecce! _____ Rides Winged Horse

Perseus and Medusa

Medusa was once a young woman with lovely hair. She thought she was more beautiful than the goddess Minerva. This made Minerva so angry that she changed Medusa's hair into hissing snakes, and anyone who looked directly at Medusa was turned into stone.

Perseus undertook to kill Medusa, with the help of Mercury's winged sandals and a bronze shield given to him by Minerva. To avoid looking directly at Medusa, he used his shield to catch her reflection and cut off her head as she slept. As Perseus watched in amazement, Pegasus, the winged horse, sprang from Medusa's blood.

The people could now walk freely in the countryside without fear of being turned into stone.

Perseus et Medūsa

A Perseus est fīlius Iovis.
Perseus est iuvenis fortis.

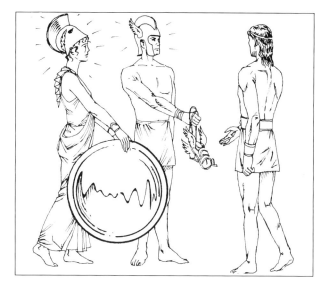

B Minerva Perseum adiuvat.
Mercurius Perseum adiuvat.

C ecce! crīnēs Medūsae!
ita vērō! serpentēs!

D Perseus Medūsam gladiō fortiter necat.
Perseus est victor.

adiuvat	*helps*		gladiō	*with a sword*
crīnēs	*hair*		Iovis	*of Jupiter*
ecce!	*look! see!*		ita vērō	*yes*
est	*is*		iuvenis	*young man*
et	*and*		Medūsae	*of Medusa*
fīlius	*son*		necat	*kills*
fortis	*brave*		serpentēs	*snakes*
fortiter	*bravely*		victor	*victor*

● Pretend you are Medusa's hairdresser. Look at the sample picture. Then using the Latin colors listed below draw and label five other snaky heads for Medusa.

A serpēns est ruber.   **D** serpēns est fulvus.

B serpēns est āter.   **E** serpēns est viridis.

C serpēns est caeruleus.

ruber	*red*		viridis	*green*
āter	*black*		fulvus	*brown*
caeruleus	*blue*		flāvus	*yellow*

F serpēns est flāvus.

- Medusa's head was the centerpiece of Minerva's shield. Design a shield which symbolizes something special about you. Follow the steps below:

  1. Fold a sheet of 12″ × 18″ coloured paper in half.
  2. Use the illustration on p.47 to draw the outline of your shield.
  3. Cut around the outline.
  4. Open up your shield and draw your own pictures on it.

- Mercury gave Perseus winged sandals. If you had winged sandals, where would they take you? What heroic feat would you accomplish? Illustrate your story.

D

Perseus and Andromeda

After killing Medusa, Perseus flew on Mercury's winged sandals over the coast of Ethiopia. He thought he saw a statue of a young woman chained to a rock. Flying closer, he noticed tears and flew down to talk to the beautiful maiden.

Andromeda told him about her misfortune. Her mother, Queen Cassiopeia, had angered the sea nymphs by boasting of her beauty. The jealous nymphs persuaded their father, Neptune, to flood the countryside, and the floods would only subside if Andromeda was sacrificed to a sea monster. So, she had been chained to the rock and left to be devoured by the monster.

King Cepheus and Queen Cassiopeia agreed to give Andromeda in marriage to Perseus if he could save her from this terrible fate. After a bloody battle, Perseus killed the monster and married Andromeda.

Perseus et Andromeda

A Perseus statuam cōnspicit.

B ēheu! Perseus est attonitus.
statua est puella.

C frūstrā Andromeda lacrimat.
nēmō adiuvat.
Perseus rem cōgitat.

D quam celerrimē Perseus mōnstrum petit.
impetus est ferōcissimus.

50

E mōnstrum dolet. multus sanguis fluit.
   opportūnē Perseus mōnstrum necat.

F Perseus rēgis fīliam servat.
   statim rēx grātiās agit.
   statim rēgīna grātiās agit.

G Perseus est marītus.
   Andromeda est uxor.

adiuvat	*helps*	nēmō	*nobody*
attonitus	*astonished*	opportūnē	*just at the right time*
cōnspicit	*catches sight of*	petit	*attacks*
dolet	*is in pain*	puella	*girl*
ēheu!	*alas!*	quam celerrimē	*as quickly as possible*
est	*is*	rēgīna	*queen*
ferōcissimus	*very ferocious*	rēgis fīliam	*princess*
fluit	*flows*	rem cōgitat	*considers the problem*
frūstrā	*in vain*	rēx	*king*
grātiās agit	*gives thanks*	sanguis	*blood*
impetus	*attack*	servat	*saves*
lacrimat	*cries*	statim	*at once*
marītus	*husband*	statua/statuam	*statue*
mōnstrum	*monster*	uxor	*wife*
multus	*much*		
necat	*kills*		

● Each picture provides the answers to two of the Latin questions below. Match each question to the appropriate picture.

____ cūr Andromeda lacrimat?   ____ quid mōnstrum necat?

____ quis dolet?   ____ ubi est Perseus?

____ cūr Perseus est attonitus?   ____ quid Perseus portat?

____ quis mōnstrum necat?   ____ ubi est mōnstrum?

A

B

C

D

attonitus	*astonished*	necat	*kills*
cūr?	*why?*	portat	*is carrying*
dolet	*is in pain*	quid?	*what?*
est	*is*	quis?	*who?*
lacrimat	*cries*	ubi?	*where?*
mōnstrum	*monster*		

- Make yourself a 3-D. First of all, find a small sturdy box (such as a shoe box). Stand it on its side so that the bottom of the box can be painted to make a background scene. Then make characters and objects out of Plasticine or clay and place them on the box, in front of the background, to create a three-dimensional effect.

- Select a group of characters from the list below and write a conversation between them.

  I   Perseus and Andromeda
  II   Queen Cassiopeia and Andromeda
  III Perseus, Queen Cassiopeia, and King Cepheus
  IV   Queen Cassiopeia, King Cepheus, and Andromeda
  V   Queen Cassiopeia and King Cepheus

Phaëthon

"Let me drive the sun chariot for one day," Phaëthon begged his father Apollo.

Apollo was sorry he had promised to grant his son anything he wished. The sun god knew that he alone could control the horses pulling the chariot. He begged his son to choose anything else, but Phaëthon would not change his mind.

Apollo warned his son to follow the wheelmarks and keep the middle path. Soon after he began, though, Phaëthon became terrified and in his distress let go of the reins. The fiery chariot plunged so close to the earth that it caused great destruction.

Mother Earth prayed to Jupiter who killed Phaëthon with a lightning bolt. His body fell into a river where his sisters found it. In their grief they were changed into poplar trees growing on the river bank, and their tears became glowing beads of amber.

Phaëthōn

A Apollō est pater.
Phaëthōn est fīlius.

B Phaëthōn equōs agit, sed patrem nōn audit.

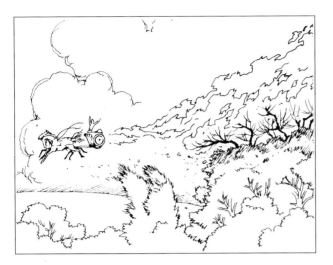

C sōl ad terram appropinquat.
sōl est ferōcissimus.
terra ardet.

D Phaëthōn est perterritus.
Phaëthōn perit.

E sorōrēs Phaëthonta lūgent.

F sorōrēs fiunt arborēs.
lacrimae fiunt sūcina.

ad terram	*to the land*	lacrimae	*tears*
agit	*drives*	lūgent	*mourn*
appropinquat	*comes close*	nōn	*not*
arborēs	*trees*	pater/patrem	*father*
ardet	*burns*	perit	*dies*
audit	*does listen to*	perterritus	*very frightened*
equōs	*horses*	sed	*but*
est	*is*	sōl	*sun*
ferōcissimus	*very ferocious*	sorōrēs	*sisters*
fīlius	*son*	sūcina	*amber*
fiunt	*become*	terra	*land*

• When you add the ending *–issimus* to certain adjectives, it changes the meaning. For example, if you change *dēnsus*, meaning "thick," to *dēnsissimus*, then the meaning changes to "very thick." Use this pattern to fill in the blanks below with the appropriate adjective from the list below:

dēnsissimus
laetissimus
ferōcissimus
līberālissimus
fortissimus
nōtissimus
īrātissimus
stultissimus

I āctor est _____ .

II amīcus est _____ .

III avārus *nōn* est _____ .

IV barbarus est _____ .

V caudex est _____ .

VI fūmus est _____ .

VII gladiātor est _____ .

VIII inimīcus est _____ .

āctor	*actor*	gladiātor	*gladiator*
amīcus	*friend*	inimīcus	*enemy*
avārus	*miser*	īrātus	*angry*
barbarus	*barbarian*	laetus	*happy*
caudex	*blockhead*	līberālis	*generous*
dēnsus	*thick*	nōn	*not*
ferōx	*ferocious*	nōtus	*famous*
fortis	*brave*	stultus	*stupid*
fūmus	*smoke*		

●   The ancient people gave the names of animals or people to groups of stars, or "constellations," according to the picture created by the stars.

Make a "spatter painting" and create your own constellation. Here's how:

1. Dip a paintbrush (or an old toothbrush) in some paint.
2. Flick the brush so the paint spatters on a sheet of 9″ × 12″ coloured paper. Let your painting dry.
3. Turn your paper around slowly until you find a dot pattern which reminds you of an animal or a person.
4. Connect the dots with a pencil to show what you have found.
5. Name your "constellation."

●   Write a story about the origin of your constellation.

●   An epitaph is an inscription on a tombstone or monument in memory of the person buried there. Often an epitaph is written in verse. Ask your librarian to help you find some epitaphs and then write one for Phaëthon. (You might also like to write an epitaph for Icarus, Actaeon, Cephalus, Midas, or Medusa.)

Find the Picture

●   Identify as many characters as possible in this picture. They all come from the stories in this book.

Sunday in the Park with Mythology

Crosswords

Fill in the mini-crossword puzzles with the correct Latin word.

I (*across*) child
(*down*) parent

	P	
I N F A N S		
	R	
	E	
	N	
	S	

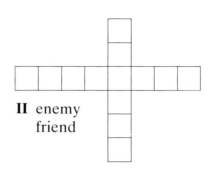

II enemy
friend

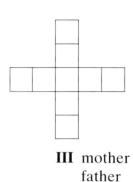

III mother
father

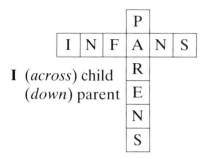

IV god
goddess

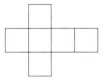

V husband
wife

VI girl
boy

P
U
E
R

VII son
daughter

F
I
L
I
A

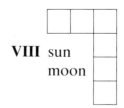

VIII sun
moon

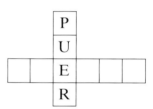

IX brother
sister

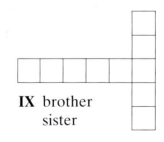

X lion
lioness

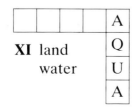

XI land
water

A
Q
U
A

XII spectator
actor

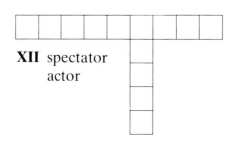

Thumbprints

columba

It is fun to make thumbprint animals. Look at the example above. Now make a thumbprint animal for each Latin word below.

aper	fēlēs	pāvō
asinus	lea	serpēns
canis	leō	
cervus	lupus	

Use your imagination to make a "mōnstrum."

On your own you might enjoy making thumbprint pictures of other Latin words you have learned.

Latinominoes

Choose a character from one of the myths in this book and write it out
horizontally. Then fit in at least three Latin words vertically making sure at least one
letter from each vertical word coincides with one from the horizontal name. For each
word, try to recite a Latin sentence from the appropriate story which includes that
word. Here is a sample Latinomino:

```
        c
        r g     n
        i l     e
        n a i   c
      M e d u s a
        s i v e t
        o e r
        n p
        i e
        s n
          t
          e
          s
```

What Is Missing?

What is missing from each picture? The title below gives you a clue.

Baucis et Philēmōn

Diāna et Actaeōn

Daphnē et Apollō

Pēgasus

Īō

Perseus et Medūsa

Phaëthōn

Perseus et Andromeda

Daedalus et Īcarus

Atalanta et Hippomenēs

Cephalus et Procris

Midas

Mythological Banners

Here is a banner for *Perseus and Medusa*.

Using 18″ × 24″ coloured paper, design your own banner for each myth.

It would be fun to use the Latin story sentences to put on a play. You may like to dress up as a mythological character from the story and pantomime the actions as the Latin is read.